Beluga
Whales

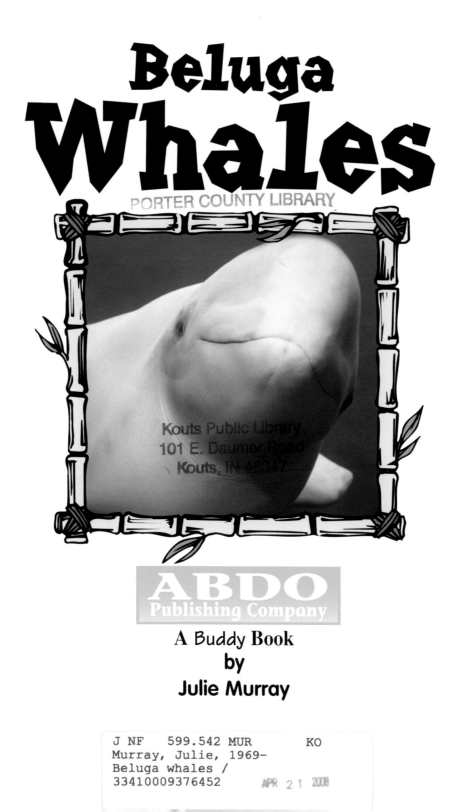

ABDO
Publishing Company

A Buddy Book
by
Julie Murray

VISIT US AT
www.abdopub.com

Published by Buddy Books, an imprint of ABDO Publishing Company, 4940 Viking Drive, Suite 622, Edina, Minnesota 55435. Copyright © 2002 by Abdo Consulting Group, Inc. International copyrights reserved in all countries. No part of this book may be reproduced in any form without written permission from the publisher.

Printed in the United States.

Edited by: Christy DeVillier
Contributing Editors: Matt Ray, Michael P. Goecke
Graphic Design: Maria Hosley
Image Research: Deborah Coldiron
Cover Photograph: Minden Pictures
Interior Photographs: Brandon Cole Marine Photography, Minden Pictures

Library of Congress Cataloging-in-Publication Data

Murray, Julie, 1969-
  Beluga Whales/Julie Murray.
    p. cm. — (Animal kingdom)
  Summary: Introduces the habitat and characteristics of the beluga whale.
  ISBN 1-57765-709-8
    1. White whale—Juvenile literature. [1. White whale. 2. Whales.] I. Title. II. Animal kingdom
(Edina, Minn.)

QL737.C433 M87 2002
599.5'42—dc21

                                                    2001053399

Contents

Sea Mammals

Whales, dolphins, and porpoises are cetaceans. Cetaceans are mammals that live in the water. Other sea mammals are seals, walruses, and sea lions.

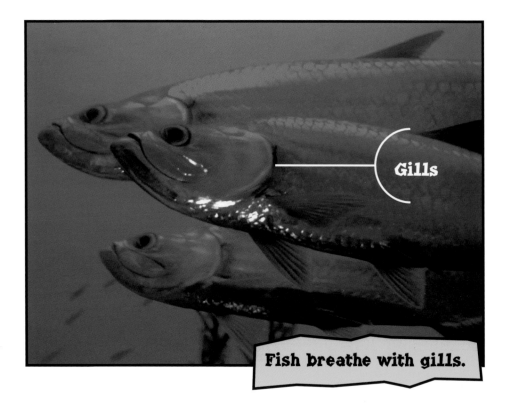

Gills

Fish breathe with gills.

Sea mammals are very different from fish. Fish have gills for breathing underwater. Instead of gills, mammals use lungs for breathing air. Whales and all other mammals cannot breathe underwater like fish.

What else do mammals have in common? Mammals are born alive instead of hatching from eggs. Female mammals make milk for their babies to drink. Apes, dogs, mice, and people are mammals, too.

Mammals come in all shapes and sizes.

Beluga Whales

There are many kinds of whales. There are sperm whales, beaked whales, rorquals, and white whales. Beluga whales are white whales.

The beluga is the only whale with a true neck. So, the beluga can move its head from side to side.

These white whales like being around each other. Belugas eat, play, and travel together in groups, or pods. Living in pods helps to keep belugas safe from predators. Two predators of the beluga are killer whales and polar bears.

A pod of beluga whales.

What They Look Like

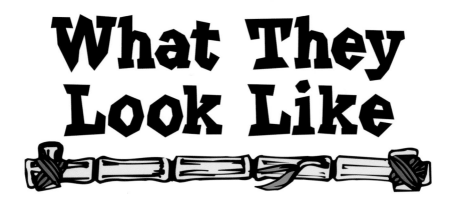

Beluga whales are smaller than many other kinds of whales. Adult belugas commonly weigh about 3,000 pounds (1,361 kg). They can grow as long as 15 feet (5 m).

Male beluga whales are bigger than the females.

Adult belugas are white all over.
They have powerful tails for swimming.
Belugas have two front flippers, one
on each side. Flippers help whales turn
different ways. And all whales have
blowholes for taking in air. The beluga's
blowhole is on top of its head.

A whale's blowhole has a
flap to keep out water.

Sea Canaries

Sailors used to call beluga whales "sea canaries." These white whales whistle, chirp, and squeal. This is how belugas communicate or "talk," with each other.

Where They Live

Beluga whales live in icy waters of the far north. They live along the shores of Alaska, Canada, Russia, and Norway. During the summer, beluga whales go where rivers spill into the sea. Some belugas may swim up a warm river, too.

Beluga whales have fat, or blubber, that keeps them warm in icy water.

A pod of whales

How do whales find their way in the deep, dark water? They make sounds, then listen to the echoes. The echoes tell them the size and shape of what is ahead. This is called echolocation. Echolocation helps whales find food, too.

Echolocation helps beluga whales find food.

Eating

Beluga whales have teeth. But belugas do not chew their food. They use their teeth to catch food. These mammals mostly eat fish and squid. They may feed on clams and octopuses, too. Belugas in the wild may eat about 15 pounds (7 kg) of food a day. That is more than two tons (1,814 kg) a year!

A beluga whale has about 40 peg-shaped teeth.

Beluga Calves

Baby whales are called calves. A beluga female commonly has one calf every three years.

A newborn beluga calf is five feet (1.5 m) long. The brownish-gray calf can swim right away. It drinks its mother's milk for about one year. The mother keeps her calf close to protect it.

A beluga whale with her calf.

Important Words

blowhole the hole on a whale's head used for taking in air.

cetacean a water mammal that has flippers, a tail, and one or two blowholes.

communicate to give and receive information. Talking is one way people communicate.

echolocation using sound and echoes to learn the shape and size of objects ahead.

flipper a flat, paddle-shaped body part that cetaceans use for swimming.

mammal most living things that belong to this special group have hair, give birth to live babies, and make milk to feed their babies.

predator an animal that hunts and eats other animals.

Web Sites

Zoom Whales: Beluga Whale

www.zoomdinosaurs.com/subjects/whales/
species/Beluga.shtml
Have fun learning more about beluga whales
through activities and games.

The Whale Center of New England

www.whalecenter.org
This site features whale sounds, pictures, and
ways to help endangered whales.

Beluga Whales

www.uvm.edu/whale/BelugaWhales.html
Plenty of facts on beluga whales can be found
here.

Index